WHERE IS THE GAS?

MARLA CONN

Photo Glossary

 balloon

 bowl

 can

 lake

 tea kettle

 tire

High Frequency Words:

- gas
- in
- is
- the
- where

Where is the gas?

4

balloon

Gas is in the **balloon.**

Where is the gas?

tea kettle

Gas is in the **tea kettle**.

Where is the gas?

Gas is in the **tire**.

Where is the gas?

10

lake

Gas is in the lake.

Where is the gas?

Gas is in the **can**.

14

bowl

Gas is in the **bowl**.

Activity

1. Go back and read the book with a partner.

2. Make a list of all the objects from the photo glossary.

3. Discuss where the gas can be found on each page.

4. Find all of the examples of gas made from water or water vapor.

5. Fill in the chart on a separate piece of paper.

I can see gas in	I cannot see gas in
the_____.	the_____.
the_____.	the_____.
the_____.	the_____.